COOKBOOK

ELDORADO GRILL
COOKBOOK

Southwestern Cuisine

Kevin Tubb

Itchy Cat Press • Blue Mounds, Wisconsin

Itchy Cat Press
A Division of Flying Fish Graphics
5452 Highway K
Blue Mounds, Wisconsin 53517

Designed and produced by Flying Fish Graphics, Blue Mounds, Wisconsin
Printed in Korea

Photographs by Ken P. Nikolai

Library of Congress Control Number: 2004112732

ISBN 0-9761450-0-6

Itchy
Cat
Press

Contents

Acknowledgments

This book has become a reality in part because of my partners at Food Fight, Inc. and in part because of my years in the industry. I have wanted to do a book for a while, and I am very happy to see that it has happened.

This partnership has been good for all parties involved. I would like to thank Peder Moren and Monty Schiro for giving me the opportunity to do what I wanted with the food. I hope that they are as happy as I am with the way Eldorado Grill has turned out. We have all learned from the experience and after six years, I think we can call the restaurant a success. Let's just hope the book is also.

I'd also like to thank everyone at Food Fight, Inc. And thanks to Joey Connaughty (the Task Master) for all her hard work throughout this project and for keeping this book on a time line.

If you have been in this business, you know that it's not easy on anyone. Long hours and hard work are the name of the game. I'd like to thank my family—Josie, Dylon and Walker—for their support and sacrifices over the past years so I was able to make this restaurant happen.

Thanks to all of the great staff over the years (front and back of the house) and all their hard work. It takes good people to make a good restaurant. Some of their recipes are here and there throughout this book. A very special thanks to Maria for her hard work and dedication to her job. She has played a big part in the consistency of the food at Eldorado Grill. Thanks and good luck to you all.

Thanks to Chef Raymond Tatum. He was the finest chef I ever worked for. I learned more from him in two years than anyone I had worked with in all other years combined. He would show you anything you asked and tell you exactly why he did it that way. One of the great chefs of the Southwest.

Thank you to Caroline Beckett and Frank Sandner of Flying Fish Graphics for all their hard work and vision in helping to create the look and feel of this book. I think you really captured the essence of Eldorado. It was a pleasure to work with you both. And to Joyce Link for her editing expertise, in between taste testings of the tequila cocktails.

And thanks to Peder and Monty for helping me get my CD recorded. This was a personal project that meant a lot to me. It would not have been possible without their personal and financial support. It was recorded between payrolls and inventory in six days, back home in Austin, Texas, July 19–25, 2004.

Sincerely,

Kevin Tubb

The Classic Eldorado Grill Menu

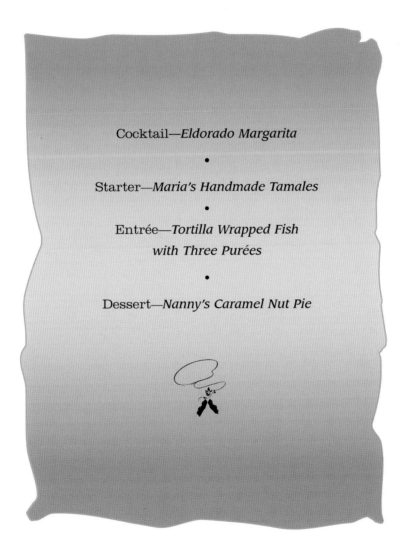

Cocktail—*Eldorado Margarita*

•

Starter—*Maria's Handmade Tamales*

•

Entrée—*Tortilla Wrapped Fish
with Three Purées*

•

Dessert—*Nanny's Caramel Nut Pie*

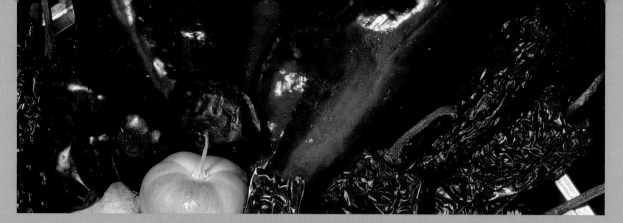

TIPS & HOW TO'S

Chile Purées

This is EASY! Soak chiles in warm water until completely soft. Sometimes I add different spices with the chiles and water if I want a certain flavor. But most of the time, water is fine. Make sure your chiles are not hot (temperature-wise, that is) when you're ready to blend them.

Put the soaked chiles in a blender. Fill the blender no more than 3/4 full, since the chiles soak up a lot of water. However, make sure you have enough water, gradually adding more, as needed, while blending until smooth.

Ancho Purée

5 ancho chiles, seeded and stemmed
1 cup hot water

Soak the chiles until soft, about an hour.

Put in blender and purée until smooth. Add a little water if needed. This should be pourable, but not too thin.

Yield: 1 1/2 cups

Roasting and Peeling Chiles and Peppers

There are a lot of different methods for roasting and peeling. This is how I like to do it.

You'll need an open flame gas stove or a small utility torch. Turn your burner on high and place chile or pepper directly on the flame. Hold the chile with a pair of tongs, and rotate the chile constantly, blistering the skin on all sides. Turning is key—it keeps the meat of the chile or pepper fresh. The biggest mistake people make is not turning the chile often enough. This makes the meat of the pepper too soft and difficult to peel.

After you have blistered the chile or pepper until it's black all over, place it in an ice bath (water with ice) to stop the cooking process. This will also help the skin come off easier.

Remove the chile or pepper from the water after it has cooled completely. Peel off the blistered skin under cool running water. Cut a slit in the chile or pepper. Rinse the seeds out. Be careful not to tear the flesh if you're making chiles rellenos. If you're using the pepper for strips or a purée, it makes no difference if it tears.

Spices

I highly recommend buying spices whole and grinding them as you need them. This way they keep their flavor much longer and really make a difference in your recipes. You can grind spices in a coffee mill or in a dry blender. (Make sure blender is completely dry before grinding spices.)

If you do a lot of cooking, you should use a separate grinder just for spices. It makes a world of difference.

These recipes use freshly ground spices and may vary a little if you are using pre-ground spices.

Grilling Fish

Grilling fish is easy. Here are a few simple rules:

1. Make sure your grill is hot!
2. Oil your fish generously.
3. Don't turn the fish too soon. It will stick to the grill.
4. Let the fish cook for 5–6 minutes on one side
   before flipping.

5. I keep a spray bottle filled with vegetable oil.
   If you do a lot of grilling, it's a must-have.
   Spray grill with oil before putting on your fish.

Blackening Tomatoes and Tomatillos

Peeling Tomatillos

Don't be afraid to let tomatoes or tomatillos get black. They will look burned, and they are, but that's what changes their flavor and consistency.

Coat the tomatoes or tomatillos with vegetable oil. Put them under the broiler on high and blacken until they get very dark—black.

Soak tomatillos in warm water while you peel them. The skin comes off easily when they're wet. The skin of a tomatillo is like a cornhusk and must be removed.

Preparing Tortillas for Rolling and Grilling Enchiladas

Heat about 1 inch of oil hot in a skillet. Place each corn tortilla in hot oil until soft; about 5–10 seconds on each side. Repeat process, stacking tortillas on a plate until you have enough for your recipe.

The tortillas should be well soaked and soft. Cover with plastic wrap and set aside until you're ready to roll.

Lay out tortillas and fill each with your choice of filling. Roll up and place in container. Chill in refrigerator for at least an hour before grilling. You can keep these in the refrigerator for a few days, well wrapped.

Recipes for fillings include *Flaco's Grilled Lobster, Shrimp and Crab Enchiladas*, page 80, *Red Chile Enchiladas*, page 81, *Smoked Chicken Enchiladas*, page 85, *Pasilla Chicken Enchiladas*, 104, and *Cheese and Spinach Enchiladas*, 105.

Chile Flakes

I refer to chile flakes in a lot of recipes. This process is for dried chiles only.

Remove stems and seeds.
Heat about an inch of vegetable oil in a saucepan. Fry each chile for 5–15 seconds. (When you fry them, it really changes the flavor of the chiles.) Set aside and let cool for about 10 minutes. Using a food processor, chop the chiles into small pieces. Put these in a jar and they will keep for up to 4 weeks.

I use mainly ancho, pasilla and Oaxacan pasilla chiles. I also recommend getting a book on chiles to help you identify them. Sometimes grocery stores have them mislabeled. Also, try your local Mexican market for chiles.

General Tips

Pan-frying—Heat up your skillet first. Get it nice and hot, then add your cooking oil and start frying. This lets you use less oil and things won't stick nearly as much. I use a cast iron skillet whenever possible. Or you can use a stainless pan with a thick bottom.

Meats—Take meats out of the refrigerator about 10–15 minutes before cooking. This makes it easier to cook to desired temperature (medium-rare, rare, etc.). If the meat has warmed a little you're not pushing the cold back and forth through it. And remember to always season your meats generously prior to grilling or pan searing.

Skillets—Do yourself a favor and get a few good skillets. Get rid of your old, cheap pans. I like cast iron, but stainless pans with thick bottoms are also fine. I stay away from aluminum unless they are lined with stainless inside.

Knives—Get yourself a good knife, and keep it sharp. An 8-inch chef's knife is a good start.

Stocks—When using stock for a recipe, make sure it has good flavor and body. You have to start with good stock to get a good finished product. Buying seasoned stocks from the grocery store is fine.

Cornstarch Mixture and Roux are used for thickening sauces, soups, and gravies.

Cornstarch Mixture

1/3 cup cornstarch
1/4 cup water

Mix cornstarch and water. When you are ready to use it, make sure mixture is stirred thoroughly.

Yield: 1/2 cup

Roux

1 stick unsalted butter
1 loose cup flour

(Pronounced *roo*.) Melt butter in medium saucepan. Add flour a little at a time, stirring constantly. Cook on very low heat until slightly browned, stirring occasionally.

Refrigerate roux for up to 2 weeks. If cold, warm roux in the microwave for 10 seconds to soften it.

Yield: 1 cup

Eldorado's Original House Salsa

2 cups canned, diced tomatoes
*   (good quality)*
1/4 small red onion, chopped
1/4 small white onion, chopped
1 scallion, chopped
1/8 teaspoon cumin
1/2 fresh jalapeño, stemmed but
*   not seeded*
1/2 teaspoon salt
1 teaspoon freshly squeezed lime juice
1/2 teaspoon white vinegar
1 clove garlic
1/2 Oaxacan chile, seeded and diced
1 tablespoon chopped cilantro

Place all ingredients in blender. Blend until semi-smooth, with a little chunk left in it.

Refrigerate for at least 2 hours before serving. Best if chilled for 24 hours.

Yield: 3 cups

SALSAS, SAUCES & PURÉES

Pineapple Poblano Salsa

This is tasty on chicken, fish or pork.

1 fresh pineapple, diced into
    1/4-inch cubes
1/4 bunch cilantro, stemmed and
    chopped (about 3 tablespoons)
2 fresh poblano peppers, roasted, peeled,
    seeded and sliced into thin strips
1 teaspoon cracked pepper
Pinch of salt

Gently toss all ingredients together in a bowl. Refrigerate for up to 5 days.

For a better pineapple flavor, serve slightly chilled, but not cold.

Yield: 2 cups

Chad's Sweet and Sour Tomatillo Salsa

Use on fish, pork or chicken.

10 tomatillos, peeled and diced
4 large Roma tomatoes, diced
1 red bell pepper, diced
1 poblano pepper, thinly sliced
1 bunch scallions, chopped
1/2 bunch cilantro, chopped
1 cup pickled red onion, chopped
    (see Garnishes, page 43)
2 tablespoons cider vinegar
2 serrano peppers, thinly sliced
1/4 cup honey
Salt and pepper to taste

Mix all ingredients together in a bowl. Refrigerate overnight before serving.

Yield: 2 1/2 cups

Tomato Salsa

Eat as a tomato salad or as a garnish for pork, chicken, fish, beef, lamb—well, just about anything. If you like a more Southwestern flavor, mix in 1 tablespoon of pasilla or ancho chile flakes.

5 fresh Roma tomatoes, halved
   and sliced
2 scallions, thinly sliced
3–4 fresh sage leaves, chopped
2 cloves garlic, minced
1 1/2 tablespoons olive oil
1 tablespoon balsamic vinegar
1 teaspoon black pepper
1/4 teaspoon salt

Gently mix all ingredients together in a bowl. Serve slightly chilled or at room temperature.

The flavors are more natural and pronounced when the salsa has had time to warm slightly.

Yield: 1 1/2-2 cups

Blackened Tomato and Poblano Salsa

Great with your favorite tortilla chips. Also good with chicken, fish, pork tacos, enchiladas or burritos.

3 pounds Roma tomatoes
1 tablespoon vegetable oil
1/2 small yellow onion, diced
1 poblano pepper, thinly sliced
2 cloves garlic, minced
1/4 bunch cilantro, chopped
3 tablespoons white vinegar
1 teaspoon salt
1/2 teaspoon ground black pepper

Coat tomatoes very lightly with oil. Place in ovenproof pan and blacken under broiler until very dark on one side—yes, burned.

Let cool slightly and purée in blender. Pour purée over the remaining ingredients in a large mixing bowl. Toss mixture.

Refrigerate for 24 hours before serving.

Yield: 4 cups

Maria's Roasted Tomatillo Chile Arbol

Great for chips, tacos, eggs or as a garnish. This is very spicy, but delicious!

1 pound tomatillos, peeled and washed
5 chile arbol
5 cloves garlic, peeled
2 tablespoons vegetable oil, divided
1/4 yellow onion, diced
1/4 bunch cilantro, chopped
Salt to taste

Preheat broiler.

Place tomatillos, chile arbol and garlic in an oven-ready broiler pan. Coat with one tablespoon of oil. Under the broiler, brown one side only until very dark.

Cool to room temperature. Combine tomatillo mixture with onion, cilantro and salt in a blender and pulse until semi-smooth.

Heat remaining oil in saucepan until it starts to smoke. Pour in the sauce, searing it in the oil. **Be careful** not to burn yourself. This will splash a lot, but it's necessary to bring out the flavor of the salsa.

Remove from heat; serve at either room temperature or chilled.

Yield: 2 cups

Pico De Gallo

Serve with tortilla chips or use as a garnish.

5 large tomatoes, diced
1 large yellow onion, diced
2 jalapeños, finely diced
1/2 bunch cilantro, stemmed and chopped
3 tablespoons lime juice
1/2 teaspoon salt
1/2 cup water

Combine all ingredients in a mixing bowl and stir gently. Store in refrigerator for up to 1 week.

Yield: 3 cups

Salsa Verde

Use for fish, chicken or pork. Also great with enchiladas, burritos or tortilla chips.

2 pounds tomatillos, peeled and washed
1 tablespoon vegetable oil
1/2 medium yellow onion, chopped
2 garlic cloves, peeled
1 jalapeño, stemmed
1 teaspoon salt
1 bunch cilantro, including stems
about 1 cup water
additional salt to taste

Bring 1 1/2 gallons of water to a boil. Add tomatillos. Turn off the heat and cover. Let stand for 10 minutes. Drain and let cool.

While tomatillos are soaking, heat oil in a small skillet. Add onion, garlic, jalapeño and salt. Sauté until golden brown.

Working in batches, fill blender 2/3 full with cooled tomatillos, some of the sauté mixture and some of the cilantro. Blend until very smooth, adding water as needed. Repeat this process until all ingredients are used. Combine all batches into 1 large bowl. Stir well; add salt to taste.

Yield: 6 cups

Chipotle Purée

This gives a smokey, hot barbeque flavor. Use it as a hot sauce, or add it to other cream sauces for more flavor. This makes a rich red-orange purée.

1 can (7-ounces) chipotle peppers
1/4–1/2 cup water (just enough to
*   blend peppers smooth, not runny;*
*   start with 1/4 cup)*

Mix ingredients together in blender at high speed until smooth.

Store in refrigerator for up to 2 weeks.

Yield: 1 cup

Black Bean Purée

I use this purée as a color accent because of its rich purple.

1/2 cup cooked black beans, or
*   canned is fine*
Salt to taste
1/2–1 cup water (start with 1/2 cup)

Place all ingredients in a blender and blend at high speed until smooth. Refrigerate for up to 2 weeks.

Yield: 1 1/2 cups

Chad's Tomatillo (Green) BBQ Sauce

This is great on chicken, pork or fish.

15 tomatillos, peeled
2–3 teaspoons vegetable oil
1/2 yellow onion, chopped
2 cloves garlic, minced
1 bunch green onions (tops only), chopped
1 bunch cilantro, stemmed and chopped
1/2 cup white vinegar
7 ounces (half bottle) ketchup
1 tablespoon Dijon mustard
1 cup brown sugar
1/8 cup molasses
1/2 cup sugar
1/2 cup honey
3 jalapeños, chopped
2 poblanos, chopped

Blacken tomatillos under broiler for 15 minutes or until good and black (don't be afraid to burn them). When blackened, cool them to room temperature or chill.

Heat oil in a skillet. Add onions and garlic and sauté until lightly caramelized. Let cool.

Purée cooled tomatillos, onion mixture and remaining ingredients in blender.

Note: Continuous heat will turn this mixture brown. Heat only immediately before serving.

Yield: 1 1/2 quarts

Achiote Purée

Use as a rub for fish, chicken or pork. It's great to use with other sauces, like Lime Cream (page 35) or Salsa Verde (page 27).

2 ounces achiote paste*
1/3 cup distilled white vinegar (or more as needed)
1/2 tablespoon salt
3 cloves garlic, minced
1/2 teaspoon coriander
1/2 teaspoon allspice
1/2 teaspoon white pepper

*You can find this in latino grocery stores.

Purée all ingredients in blender until smooth. Use more vinegar, if needed for consistency, to purée.

Yield: 1 cup

Roasted Chile Pasilla Sauce

This is a great sauce to use on steak, pork, chicken, enchiladas or meat loaf.

2 quarts chicken stock
5 cloves garlic
1/2 cup pasilla chile flakes
1/2 cup roux (page 17)

Add chicken stock, garlic and chile pasilla flakes to a large stockpot. Bring to a boil; lower heat and let simmer until liquid has reduced by a third.

Add roux; stir constantly and briskly with whisk to incorporate roux, not leaving any lumps.

Let simmer for a little while longer; stir constantly. Look for the consistency of a brown gravy.

Yield: 4 cups

Ancho Sauce

Great for steak, pork or chicken.

2 cups ancho purée (page 9)
2 cups chicken stock or water
1 tablespoon cider vinegar
3 tablespoons honey
1 tablespoon freshly squeezed lime juice

Place all ingredients in medium sauce pan. Bring to a low simmer and reduce by one fourth.

It is important not to boil. Stir often.

Yield: 3 cups

Pineapple Pasilla Chile Sauce

Use this on fish, chicken or pork.

1 tablespoon brown sugar
1 can (48 ounces) pineapple juice
3 tablespoons pasilla jalapeño
1/4 cup cornstarch
1/8 cup water

In a dry saucepan over medium heat, caramelize (begin to melt) brown sugar. Don't let it burn.

Pour pineapple juice into caramelized sugar. Add jalapeño. Simmer for 30 to 50 minutes.

When it has reduced by half, mix cornstarch with water and add to saucepan. Stir vigorously with whisk so you don't have lumps. Simmer for 5 minutes.

Yield: about 3 cups

Pineapple, Mango and Oaxacan Chile Sauce

Use with chicken, pork or fish.

1 tablespoon brown sugar
1 ounce tequila
1 can (48 ounces) pineapple juice
1 can (27 ounces) mango slices,
*   syrup drained off*
1 Oaxacan chile, seeded and cut into
*   thin strips*
1/4 cup corn starch
1/8 cup water

In a dry saucepan over medium heat, caramelize (begin to melt) brown sugar. Don't let it burn.

With caution, add tequila. It may spatter or flame up. Add pineapple juice, mangos and chile strips; simmer for about 30 minutes; reduce liquid by half.

Stir vigorously with whisk, breaking up mangos into smaller pieces.

Mix water and cornstarch together and slowly mix into sauce while stirring with a whisk so you don't create lumps. This gives the sauce a nice shimmer and keeps it from weeping when you put the sauce on plates.

Yield: 6 cups

Lime Cream Sauce

This is great on chicken, pork, lamb or fish.

1 quart chicken stock
2 cups heavy cream
2 ounces freshly squeezed lime juice
3 tablespoons roux (page 17)

Combine chicken stock, heavy cream and lime juice in a large saucepan. Bring to a boil. Reduce heat and whisk in roux, stirring vigorously to remove all lumps.

Simmer and reduce the sauce by a third. Be careful not to reduce to a thick gravy.

Yield: 3 cups

Roasted Garlic Green Chile Sauce

This is a fine sauce for pork, chicken, steaks, tamales or enchiladas.

1 quart chicken stock
3 cloves garlic
1 1/2 tablespoons roux (page 17)
1 1/2 cups New Mexico green chiles
1/2 small bunch cilantro
3/4 teaspoon salt

Combine chicken stock and garlic in a large saucepan. Bring to a boil. Reduce heat and simmer until sauce is reduced by one third.

Pour through strainer into another saucepan, pushing softened garlic through strainer with the back of a spoon.

Bring sauce back to a boil; add roux, stirring vigorously with whisk to remove all lumps. Simmer for about 10 minutes. Remove from heat.

Let cool 20–30 minutes. Combine sauce, chiles, cilantro and salt in a blender. Blend until smooth.

Heat when ready to serve.

Yield: 3 1/2 cups

Chipotle Bleu Butter

Seared Steak with Chipotle Bleu Butter is a signature dish at Eldorado. This can be also used on bread, potatoes, vegetables, or just about anything.

1 pound unsalted butter, softened
1 pound bleu cheese, crumbled
1/3 cup Dijon mustard
1/3 cup chipotle purée (page 28)

Using the paddle attachment on your mixer, whip butter until very light and fluffy.

Add remaining ingredients and mix well. Put butter mix in bowl and refrigerate. You can also roll in waxed paper and store in freezer for 90 days.

Prepare some steaks and top each steak with 1 tablespoon of Chipotle Bleu Butter.

Yield: This will cover a heck of a lot of steaks.

Buttermilk Gravy

Serve this on meat loaf, mashed potatoes, corn bread, Chicken Fried Steak (page 96) or biscuits.

3 slices bacon, diced
1/2 yellow onion, finely diced
1 teaspoon salt
1 tablespoon black pepper
2 tablespoons butter
4 tablespoons flour
1 cup half-and-half
2 cups buttermilk

Brown bacon and onions in a saucepan.

Add salt and pepper. Add butter and let it melt, then add flour.

Stir well while adding the half-and-half. Simmer on low heat for 4–5 minutes, stirring or whisking constantly.

Add the buttermilk. Simmer for another minute. Remove from heat.

Yield: 3 cups

Chipotle Remoulade

This goes great with Southwestern Fish Cakes (page 65).

1 cup mayonnaise
1/2 tablespoon freshly squeezed
    lemon juice
3 tablespoons finely diced red onion
1 clove garlic, minced
1 tablespoon chipotle purée (page 28)
1/2 tablespoon finely chopped capers
1 teaspoon salt
1/4 teaspoon black pepper
1/2 tablespoon Tabasco

Stir all ingredients together in small mixing bowl. Chill and store in refrigerator for up to 5 days.

Yield: 1 1/2 cups

GARNISHES & EXTRAS

Ancho Pineapple Chutney

This is an intensely sweet garnish for chicken or pork. Use on Ancho Corn Bread Muffins (page 47) or toast for breakfast.

1 fresh pineapple
1/2 cup honey
1 teaspoon sesame oil
1 cup ancho purée (page 9)
1/4 cup cider vinegar
1 cup pineapple juice

Dice pineapple into 1/4–1/2 inch cubes.

Combine all ingredients in a shallow saucepan. Simmer until all liquid is completely gone and sugars are caramelized, about 1 to 1 1/2 hours.

Refrigerate for 24 hours before serving. This can be stored for up to 2 weeks.

Yield: 1 1/2 cups of pineapple

Pork Marinade

In Mexico, Coke or Pepsi is used to make all kinds of dishes, especially stews. It can also be used in terrific marinades for pork, beef or chicken.

1/2 quart Pepsi
1/4 cup soy sauce
3 cloves garlic
1/2 tablespoon chile pasilla flakes
1/8 cup black pepper

Combine all ingredients in a bowl. Pour over the meat and let marinate for at least 4–5 hours, but it's best if marinated for 24 hours.

Yield: Marinates about 3-5 pounds of meat

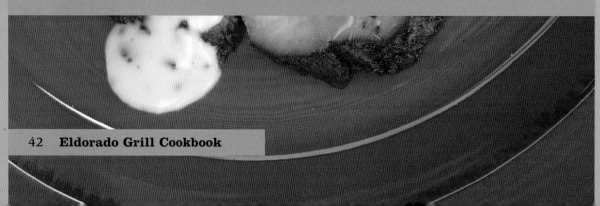

Pickled Red Onions

This is a simple but flashy garnish—it's bright pink.

1 red onion, thinly sliced
2 cups distilled white vinegar

Place onions in a bowl. Cover with vinegar. Chill for a minimum of 2 hours, preferably overnight.

Yield: 1 cup

Chorizo Frying Rub

You can make this recipe without the chorizo for a vegetable corn rub. Great for fish, chicken or pork.

7 1/2 ounces chorizo, casing removed
3/4 cup blue cornmeal
1/4 cup flour
1/4 cup brown sugar
1 1/2 tablespoons kosher salt
3/4 tablespoon black pepper
1/2 tablespoon coriander
1/2 tablespoon cumin
1/4 cup vegetable oil

Heat a cast iron skillet or sauté pan. Add chorizo and cook, breaking it into small pieces with a spoon or fork, for a texture like ground beef.

Brown well and transfer to a fine strainer to drain oil and cool.

Combine all remaining ingredients in a shallow pan. Knead in the chorizo, breaking into small pieces and incorporating it into the cornmeal mixture.

Use this recipe as a breading for catfish, mahi mahi or almost any white fish. When breading the fish, oil the fillets on both sides and press them firmly into the cornmeal mixture, coating both sides completely. Fry over medium-high heat with oil, flipping after breading is crispy, about 3–4 minutes. Finish in the oven at 425 degrees for 8–10 minutes.

Yield: Covers about 8 fish

Blackening Spice Rub

Use this rub for blackened catfish, pork, beef or chicken.

6 tablespoons dark chile powder
1 tablespoon ground cumin
1 tablespoon ground coriander
1 tablespoon ground white pepper
1 tablespoon dried marjoram
1 tablespoon salt
1/2 tablespoon ground allspice,
1/2 tablespoon ground cayenne pepper

Combine all ingredients in shallow container with lid. Store for as long as you like. This mixture will lose some potency after a while, especially if you buy the spices pre-ground. See spice tips on page 11.

Yield: Covers about 3 pounds of meat

Potato and Chorizo Stuffing

This is a terrific stuffing for quail, chicken, pork or turkey.

1 pound mild chorizo, browned and drained
3 large potatoes, peeled and steamed until soft

Heat a cast iron skillet or sauté pan. Add chorizo and cook, breaking it into small pieces with a spoon or fork, for a texture like ground beef.

Brown well and transfer to a fine strainer to drain oil and cool.

Mix prepared chorizo and potatoes. (You can boil the potatoes, but steaming gives more consistent results. I recommend steaming for mashed potatoes and potato salad. The potatoes won't get water-logged if they are over-cooked.)

Chill before stuffing the meat.

Yield: 6 cups.

Ancho Corn Bread Muffins

Serve with pineapple chutney. The muffins can be cut in half and grilled. They're great with steak or pork.

3 cups all-purpose flour
1 cup yellow cornmeal
1 1/4 cups sugar
1 1/2 tablespoons baking powder
1 teaspoon salt
1/2 tablespoon cinnamon
4 large ancho chiles, seeded (divided)
Zest of 1 lime
1/2 cup buttermilk
2 eggs
3/4 cup vegetable oil

Preheat oven to 350 degrees. Combine flour, cornmeal, sugar, baking powder, salt and cinnamon in a large mixing bowl.

Place 2 ancho chiles, lime zest and buttermilk in a blender and purée until smooth. Pour into a medium bowl. Whisk in eggs and vegetable oil. Chop remaining ancho chiles and add to mixture.

Gradually stir the dry ingredients into the purée. Scoop mixture into muffin pan and bake until golden brown, for 20–25 minutes.

Yield: 12–18 muffins

Hotter Than the Texas Sun Menu

Cocktail—*Smoking Gun*

•

Starter—*Stuffed Oaxacan Chiles with*
Sesame Vinaigrette and Pickled Red Onions

•

Entrée—*Chile Rubbed Pork with*
Ancho Lime Cream,
Ancho Pineapple Chutney and Corn Cake

•

Dessert—*Ancho Pecan Pie*

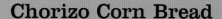

Chorizo Corn Bread

2 cups yellow cornmeal
1 cup flour
1/4 cup sugar
1 tablespoon baking powder
3/4 teaspoon baking soda
pinch of salt
3/4 cup milk
1 1/4 cups canola oil
2 eggs
1/2 cup grated cheddar cheese
1 fresh finely chopped jalapeño
1 pound chorizo sausage, cooked and
    drained

Preheat oven to 325 degrees.

Mix all dry ingredients together in large bowl.

Mix wet ingredients separately in a large bowl along with chorizo, cheese and jalapeño.

Pour wet mixture into dry mix; combine well. Pour into 12-by-12-inch pan and bake for 25–30 minutes.

Yield: 8 servings

Blue Corn Cakes

4 1/2 cups blue cornmeal
3/4 cup all-purpose flour
1 1/2 tablespoons sugar
1 1/2 teaspoons salt
1/2 teaspoon black pepper
3/4 tablespoon baking powder
3/4 tablespoon baking soda
1 3/4 cups buttermilk
4 eggs
1 small yellow onion, grated
1/3 cup vegetable oil

Combine cornmeal, flour, sugar, salt, pepper, baking powder and baking soda in a large bowl. Combine buttermilk, eggs and onion in a small mixing bowl. Mix well. Slowly add buttermilk mixture to dry ingredients and mix well.

Heat oil in cast iron skillet or sauté pan. Drop 2 tablespoons of mixture per pancake into skillet; cook like pancakes.

These corn cakes are a great garnish for many dishes.

Yield: 24–30 cakes

Seared Collard Greens

These aren't the collards you usually see. These taste great and are actually good for you.

3 bunches of collards, thick stems removed
1 cup olive oil
1/2 cup canola oil
2 tablespoons white vinegar
1 tablespoon balsamic vinegar
1 tablespoon salt
2 tablespoons black pepper
3 cloves fresh garlic
1/2 red onion, diced
1/3 cup soy sauce
1 tablespoon dried marjoram

Wash and dry collards. Cut into medium-sized pieces.

Blend all other ingredients in a blender until smooth. Lightly coat collards with dressing.

Heat a cast iron skillet very hot—about 10 minutes on medium heat. Cook collards in batches, stirring constantly while cooking until tender, 4–6 minutes. The trick is to sear the oils and flavors from the dressing into the collards.

Yield: 6 servings

Green Chile Pinto Beans

2 strips smoked bacon
1/3 yellow onion, diced
3 cloves garlic, minced
2 teaspoons salt
1 tablespoon black pepper
1/4 cup cider vinegar
1 1/2 cups green chiles, diced (canned
  is fine)
4 cups pinto beans
4 cups chicken stock

Sauté bacon in a large saucepan. When bacon is almost brown, add onions, garlic, salt and pepper. Cook until brown. Pour in vinegar and chiles. Sauté for 2 minutes.

Add beans and chicken stock to saucepan; bring to a boil. Reduce heat and simmer, loosely covered, until beans are tender, about 1 hour.

Yield: 2 1/2 quarts

STARTERS-SOUPS, SALADS & APPETIZERS

Tortilla Soup

2 pounds Roma tomatoes
4 cloves garlic, minced
2 tablespoons vegetable oil plus
    1/2 cup, divided
1/2 large yellow onion, chopped
1 fresh jalapeño, chopped
3 quarts chicken stock
12 yellow corn tortillas, divided
3 ancho chiles, seeded and finely chopped
2 pasilla chiles, seeded and finely chopped
1/2 tablespoon dark chile powder
2 handfuls of tortilla chips
2 tablespoons chipotle purée
1/2 pound shredded Monterey Jack cheese

Coat Roma tomatoes with 1 tablespoon vegetable oil. Use the broiler to blacken tomatoes on both sides (10 minutes on each side). They should be very black—as if you are burning them.

Heat 1/2 tablespoon vegetable oil in sauté pan. Add onion, garlic and jalapeño and sauté until golden brown and soft. Set aside.

Once tomatoes are blackened and cooled, place in blender. Add sauté mix and purée until smooth.

Heat 1/2 tablespoon vegetable oil in a large saucepan until it's smoking. Add blender mix (**this will splash, so be careful**) and immediately add chicken stock.

Tear 6 yellow corn tortillas into 2-inch pieces and add them to stock mixture. Add ancho and pasilla chiles and chili powder. Bring to a boil and reduce heat. Simmer for about 45 minutes.

Add tortilla chips and chipotle purée. Remove from heat.

Cut remaining 6 corn tortillas into strips. Fry them in 1/2 cup hot vegetable oil in a small pan until crisp. Drain them on paper towels.

Put a large pinch of shredded cheese in the bottom of a soup bowl. Add soup and garnish with tortilla strips. Serve immediately.

Yield: 8–10 servings

Sopa de Chihuahua (the region, not the dog)

1 tablespoon butter
1/2 tablespoon vegetable oil
1 large yellow onion, diced
4 portabella mushroom caps, sliced
1/2 tablespoon salt
1/2 tablespoon black pepper (coarse or
*   fresh cracked)*
1/2 pound ham, diced medium
3 quarts chicken stock
1 tablespoon pasilla flakes or
*   2 pasilla chiles*
2 tablespoons dark chili powder
4 cobs roasted or grilled corn, cut from cob
*   (or 2 cups frozen corn kernels)*
4 corn tortillas, torn into medium pieces
1/2 cup masa flour (or tamale masa) plus
*   1 cup water, mixed together*
Fresh avocado slices
Chopped cilantro for garnish

Heat butter and oil in 6-quart saucepan. Add onions, mushrooms, salt and pepper and sauté until dark brown. Do not burn.

Add ham and brown it. Add chicken stock, pasilla flakes, chili powder, corn, tortillas, and masa flour mix. Simmer for about 30 minutes.

Garnish with avocado slices and cilantro.

Yield: 8–10 servings

Corn Soup

2 tablespoons butter
1 teaspoon salt
1/4 teaspoon white pepper
1 clove garlic, minced
1 1/2 pounds fresh corn cut from
    the cob, or frozen is fine
1/2 gallon milk, divided
crumbled Monterey Jack cheese
crumbled tortilla chips

Melt the butter. Mix in salt, pepper and garlic.

If the corn is frozen, make sure it's thawed. Blend half the corn, half the milk and all the butter mixture in a blender until very smooth.

Strain the mixture. Discard material left in the strainer.

Add the remaining ingredients. Repeat the procedure above.

Heat in a double boiler. When ready to serve, put crumbled Monterey Jack cheese in individual bowls, add the soup, and top with crumbled tortilla chips.

Yield: 6 servings

Shrimp Relish Salad

Use this relish salad to top grilled fish dishes. You can also use it on salad greens, stuffed tomatoes or avocados.

3 quarts water
juice of 1/2 lemon
1 tablespoon Tabasco sauce
1 1/2 pounds peeled and deveined shrimp
(can be frozen)
1 tablespoon olive oil
1 clove garlic, chopped
1 tablespoon chile pasilla flakes (page 15)
1/2 teaspoon salt
2 tablespoons freshly squeezed lime juice

Place water, lemon and Tabasco sauce into a 6-quart saucepan. Bring to a boil and drop in shrimp. Cook shrimp until tender; about 5 minutes.

Remove shrimp from water and chill. When chilled, chop in thirds.

Add olive oil, garlic, pasilla flakes, salt and lime juice. Toss and refrigerate for at least 1 hour.

Yield: 2 cups

Avocado Salad

Use to garnish steak, chicken or fish. Can also be served with chips.

4 semi-firm avocados
1/2 red onion, finely diced
1 teaspoon salt
1 tablespoon freshly squeezed lime juice
1 teaspoon white pepper
2 cloves garlic, chopped
1 red bell pepper, diced
1 jalapeño pepper, seeded and diced
1/4 bunch cilantro, stemmed and chopped
*   (approximately 3 tablespoons)*

Scoop avocado meat out of skin and dice into 1/2 inch cubes.

Mix all ingredients together and chill.

Yield: 2 cups

Tortilla Salad

This is a great salad. For a low-carb version, go easy on the tortilla strips.

1 pound field greens or salad greens, washed and dried
1 red pepper, seeded and sliced into thin strips
1 poblano chile, seeded and thinly sliced
1/4 red onion, thinly sliced
4 corn tortillas sliced into thin strips and fried until crispy (see tips on tortillas, page 14)
White portions from 2 large leeks, cleaned and sliced into thin strips

Toss everything together in a mixing bowl. When ready to serve, toss with about 3 ounces of Lemon-Cumin Vinaigrette Dressing (page 62). Garnish with tomato slices.

Yield: 4 servings

Pan-Fried Pork *(pictured)*
with Ancho Cream, Tomato Salsa and Green Chile Black-Eyed Peas

Lemon-Cumin Vinaigrette

You're gonna like this one a lot—it's real easy and great on mixed greens.

1/4 cup plus 1/8 cup tahini
1/2 cup freshly squeezed lemon juice
1/2 cup cider vinegar
1/2 bunch scallions
1/4 cup rice vinegar or cider vinegar
1 tablespoon sugar
1/2 tablespoon white pepper
1/2 plus 1/8 cup Dijon mustard
1/2 cup soy sauce
2 cloves garlic
1/2 tablespoon ground cumin
1 tablespoon ground coriander seed
1 cup olive oil

Put all ingredients in a blender and purée until completely smooth. This is a fantastic salad dressing!

Yield: 3 cups

Sesame Vinaigrette

This is a great dressing. I also drizzle it on Stuffed Oaxacan Chiles (page 74) at Eldorado Grill.

1/2 cup rice wine vinegar
1/3 cup honey
1 clove garlic
1 tablespoon mirin (sweet rice wine)
3/4 tablespoon sesame oil
3/4 tablespoon Asian red chile paste
Pinch of salt
1 cup canola oil

Put all ingredients except the oil in a blender and purée until smooth. While the blender is running on low speed, add the oil. Store in the refrigerator.

Yield: 2 cups

Black Beans

1 pound black beans, sorted and rinsed
1/4 cup soy sauce
2 tablespoons vegetable oil
4 cloves garlic
10 cups water (2 1/2 quarts)

Place all ingredients in 4–5 quart saucepan, leaving a little room. Bring to a boil.

Turn down to simmer. Simmer until beans are tender and liquid is almost gone, about 2 hours.

Yield: 12-14 servings

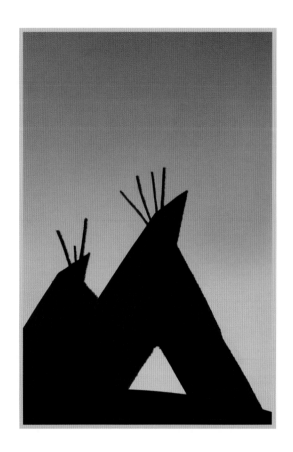

Southwestern Fish Cakes

2 pounds catfish fillets, cut into
    bite-size pieces
1 medium yellow onion, diced
1 poblano chile, diced
1/4 cup chopped cilantro
1 red pepper, seeded and chopped
1/2 cup fresh corn kernels (or
    frozen kernels)
2 cloves garlic, minced
1 tablespoon ground cumin
1 tablespoon chile pasilla flakes (page 15)
1/2 tablespoon salt
1/2 tablespoon chipotle purée (page 28)
1 teaspoon white pepper
1/2 cup mayonnaise
4 eggs, beaten
1 tablespoon Dijon mustard
1 1/2 cups flour
1/3 cup vegetable oil

Combine all ingredients except oil in a large mixing bowl and mix well.

Heat oil in cast iron skillet or sauté pan. When nice and hot, scoop 1 tablespoon of mixture per cake and drop into skillet. Cook about 8 minutes on each side, until golden brown on both sides. It should be firm when finished.

Yield: 8–12 large fish cakes

Southwestern Fish Cakes *(pictured)*
with Roasted Garlic Green Chile Sauce and
Chipotle Remoulade

Ceviche

This is a great traditional dish along the coasts of Mexico. I like to make mine with only a few types of fish, and the fish must be fresh. Use ono (wahoo), small bay scallops or halibut.

*2 1/2 pounds fresh fish, diced into
    1 inch pieces*
*1/2–1 quart fresh lime juice (to cover
    the fish completely)*
1 1/2 tablespoons salt
1 teaspoon fresh marjoram
1 ounce Triple Sec
1 ounce tequila
1/2 cup cider vinegar
Lime wedges
Pico de Gallo (page 25)
Tortilla chips

Combine first seven ingredients in a large mixing bowl. Let stand for 24–36 hours in refrigerator. Fish will turn a white color as the lime juice "cooks" the meat.

Mix well. Serve mixture in martini glass. Garnish with a lime wedge and pico de gallo, and serve with tortilla chips.

Yield: 4–6 servings

Green Chile Black-Eyed Peas

1 slice smoked, thick bacon
1/3 yellow onion, diced
3 cloves garlic, minced
2 teaspoons salt
1 tablespoon black pepper
1/4 cup cider vinegar
1 1/2 cups diced green chiles (canned
    is fine)
4 cups black-eyed peas
6 cups chicken stock

Sauté bacon in a large saucepan. When bacon is almost brown, add onion, garlic, salt and pepper. When brown, add vinegar and chiles.

Add peas and chicken stock; bring to a boil. Reduce heat and simmer, loosely covered, for about 1 hour or until peas are tender.

Yield: Makes 2 1/2 quarts

New Year's Day U
This is served in the South on January 1 as a good luck dish.

Maria's Tamale Masa

Masa is a corn-based dough used in tortillas and tamales.

4 cups tamale masa (Quaker makes one you can find in your grocery store)
1 tablespoon baking powder
1/2 teaspoon ground coriander
1/2 teaspoon ground cumin
Pinch of ground black pepper
2 teaspoons salt
1/4 teaspoon baking soda
1 1/4 to 1 3/4 cups water
3/4 cup pork fat, melted (use lard or margarine if preferred).
60 dried corn husks—you'll have extra in case they tear or are too small

If you are going to go through this much trouble, I recommend doubling or quadrupling this recipe. As is, this recipe will make about 1 dozen tamales. You can either mix this recipe by hand in a mixing bowl, or use a stand mixer with the paddle attachment.

Soak the corn husks for 20-30 minutes in warm water. Weight them with a plate to keep them submerged.

Place all ingredients except water, fat and cornhusks in a mixing bowl; mix well. Add fat and 1 cup of water. Continue mixing to get the consistency of loose cookie dough, adding water as needed to achieve this.

Arrange a corn husk so that the point of the triangle is furthest away from you. Spread 2-3 tablespoons of the masa with a spoon so that it covers most of the husk, leaving some room at the top, about 2 inches.

Once the masa is spread, put 2-3 tablespoon's of Maria's Tamale Filling (next page) up the center of the corn husk. Fold both sides of the triangle toward the middle. Then fold the top down to close that end.

Repeat process to fill all corn husks.

Place tamales upright in steamer with the open end up and steam for about 1 hour and 10 minutes. It's very hard to overcook tamales, but try not to under cook them.

Remove from heat and let stand for about 10 minutes.

Yield: 12–18 tamales

Maria's Tamale Filling

Maria Louisa Valenciano Gonzales has been making tamales from scratch since she was ten.

Most tamales are made with pork, but beef is perfectly fine. Maria's tamales are much better than mine, so we started using her recipe several years ago. Authentic!

2 pounds beef tips or pork tips
1 small onion, diced
4 cloves garlic, minced
1 tablespoon salt
1/2 tablespoon pepper
1/2 tablespoon ground allspice
2 pasilla chiles, seeded
5 ancho chiles, seeded
4 cascabel chiles, seeded
1 quart chicken stock

Brown meat tips in a large cast iron skillet or sauté pan. Add onions and garlic; cook until tender and brown.

Add spices and chiles. Cover with chicken stock; bring to a boil. Reduce heat, cover and simmer for 1 1/2 hours.

Remove cover and set aside in refrigerator until you are ready to stuff your tamales.

Yield: 16-24 tamales

Guacamole

Everybody has their own way to do this, but I like it simple and traditional.

4 ripe avocados
2 cloves garlic, chopped
1 1/2 tablespoons freshly squeezed
   lime juice
1 teaspoon salt
1/2 teaspoon ground white
   or black pepper

Place all ingredients in large mixing bowl. Use a heavy whisk or fork and mash all ingredients together.

Serve with tortilla chips.

Yield: 4–6 servings

Maria's Tamales *(pictured) with Pasilla Gravy in a poblano pepper*

Eldorado Grill Cookbook

Texas Torpedoes

Try these served with sour cream, Pico de Gallo (page 25) and fresh lime slices.

24 pickled jalapeños
1/2 pound (41–60) cooked, peeled and deveined shrimp
1 pound grated Monterey Jack cheese
24 pieces cooked bacon, slightly browned, but not crispy

Cut the stems off the jalapeños and cut a slit down one side of each.

Stuff each jalapeño with about 1 ounce of Monterey Jack cheese and one shrimp. Wrap the chile with bacon.

Put 3 or 4 on a skewer and grill for about 5 minutes on each side or bake in a preheated oven at 425 degrees for 12 to 15 minutes.

Yield: Makes 24 torpedoes

Texas Torpedoes *(pictured) with Pico de Gallo, sour cream and Chipotle Purée.*

Stuffed Ancho or Oaxacan Chiles

These are delicious but very hot if you use the Oaxacan chiles. If you like less heat, the ancho chiles are milder.

2 cups cider vinegar
1 cup brown sugar
2 tablespoons whole coriander seed
1/2 teaspoon cinnamon
1/2 teaspoon allspice
1/2 teaspoon nutmeg
12 ancho chiles or 24 Oaxacan chiles
1 1/2 pound Achiote Pork Filling (next page) or Maria's Tamale Filling (page 69)
Sesame Vinaigrette Dressing (page 62)
Pickled Red Onions (page 43)

Mix first 6 ingredients together to make a brine.

Cut a slit in the side of each chile and remove most of the seeds without tearing the chile. Put the chiles in brine and soak overnight. Make sure they are completely covered. Put a plate or cup on the chiles to weight them so they stay submerged.

When the chiles are soft, drain and then stuff each one with Achiote Pork Filling or Maria's Tamale Filling that has been shredded slightly.

Serve these at room temperature or slightly chilled. Stuff them ahead of time and take them out of the refrigerator about half an hour before serving. Put them on a platter and coat them generously with Sesame Vinaigrette Dressing. Garnish with Pickled Red Onions.

Yield: 12 servings

Achiote Pork Filling

2 1/2 pounds pork butt, cut into
    3-inch cubes
1/2 cup Achiote Purée (see page 30)
1 cup chicken stock
5 cloves garlic
1/2 tablespoon fresh ground cumin
1/2 tablespoon black pepper
1/2 tablespoon salt

Combine all ingredient in a large roasting pan or Dutch oven.

Cover and bake in a 400 degree oven for 1 hour and 45 minutes.

Uncover and bake for an additional hour or until the pork is fork-tender.

If using a crock-pot, cook on low for 5–6 hours.

Yield: 6 servings

Southwestern Meat Loaf *(pictured) with Green Chile Pinto Beans, Corn Cake and Maria's Roasted Tomatillo Chile Arbol*

Campfire Menu

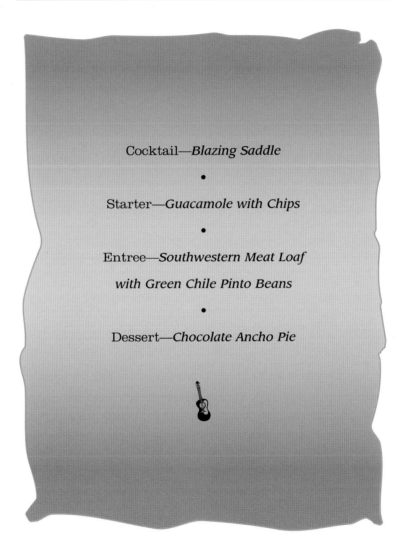

Cocktail—*Blazing Saddle*

•

Starter—*Guacamole with Chips*

•

Entree—*Southwestern Meat Loaf
with Green Chile Pinto Beans*

•

Dessert—*Chocolate Ancho Pie*

Four Cheese Chiles Rellenos

1/4 pound feta cheese, crumbled
1/4 pound white cheddar cheese, grated
1/4 pound Monterey Jack cheese, grated
1/4 pound cream cheese, softened
1/2 tablespoon freshly squeezed lime juice
3 scallions, sliced
1/2 tablespoon black pepper
6 fresh poblano peppers, roasted
        and peeled
Canola oil, as needed
4 eggs, separated
3/4 cup flour

Combine cheeses, lime juice, scallions and black pepper in a large mixing bowl.

Cut a slit into one side of each pepper. Using a spoon, stuff each pepper with 2 ounces of cheese mixture and set aside.

Heat about 1 inch of canola oil in cast iron skillet or sauté pan. While oil is heating, beat egg whites until stiff. Gently fold lightly beaten egg yolks into egg whites. Roll each chile into egg mixture, coating completely. Roll each chile in flour, coating completely.

Drop each chile into hot skillet and cook for 5–6 minutes. Remove and place on paper towel to drain excess oil.

Serve with salsa of your choice.

Yield: 6 servings

Achiote Rubbed Catfish *(pictured) with*
Shrimp Relish Salad and Lime-Cream Sauce

Flaco's Grilled Lobster, Shrimp and Crab Enchiladas

1/2 yellow onion, finely diced
4 cloves garlic, minced
1 teaspoon salt
1 teaspoon black pepper
2 tablespoons butter
1/2 pound cooked lobster meat, chopped
1/2 pound cooked crab meat, chopped
1 1/2 pound cooked shrimp, chopped
1 pound Monterey Jack cheese, grated
1/4 pound cream cheese, softened
16 corn tortillas

Heat butter in a large sauté pan. Add onions, garlic, salt and pepper.

Sauté until tender. Put sauté mix in medium bowl and set aside; let cool.

When sauté mix is cool, add remaining ingredients; mix well. Roll mixture into enchiladas. (See rolling and grilling tips on page 14.) Grill or bake at 425 degrees for 25 minutes.

Yield: 12–16 enchiladas

Red Chile Enchiladas

*1 roasted or boiled chicken, meat picked
     from the bone and shredded
1/2 cup New Mexico red chile
1/2 teaspoon salt
1/2 teaspoon black pepper
1/4 cup white vinegar
1 cup sour cream
18 corn tortillas*

Combine all ingredients in a bowl. Roll into enchiladas. (See page 14 for rolling and grilling tips.) Grill or bake at 425 degrees for 25 minutes.

Yield: 18 enchiladas

**Flaco's Grilled Lobster, Shrimp & Crab
Enchiladas** *(pictured) with Lime Cream
Sauce, Chipotle Purée and
Black Bean Purée*

K.W.'s Texas Chile

6 morita chiles, seeded
12 New Mexico red chiles, seeded
20 cascabel chiles, seeded
3 pasilla chiles, seeded
3 cups water
3/4 cup canola oil, divided
1 large onion, diced medium
5 pounds sirloin tips
6 cloves garlic, minced
1/3 cup dark chile powder
1 tablespoon black pepper
1 tablespoon salt
1 cup flour
2 cups diced green chiles (canned is fine)
5 quarts chicken stock

Place all chiles—except green chiles—in water in medium saucepan. Bring to boil; reduce heat and simmer for about 1 hour or until all chiles are tender. Strain into bowl, saving water. Place chiles aside and let cool.

When cool, place chiles in blender and purée until smooth, adding reserved chile water as needed to create a pudding consistency.

Heat 1/4 of the oil in a large stockpot. Add onions and sauté until golden brown. Add beef tips and garlic; continue to cook for about 8 minutes, stirring often and browning well.

Add all spices and simmer for 2 minutes. Add remaining oil, flour and green chiles, stirring well, until the flour coats the beef tips.

Add 1 quart of chicken stock, stirring as you add to incorporate the flour. Add remaining stock and chile purée; simmer on low heat, uncovered, for about 2 hours, stirring occasionally.

Yield: 1 1/2 gallons (but it goes fast!)

Lemon Jalapeño Chicken Breast

I recommend serving this with Blackened Tomato and Poblano Salsa (page 23), or Pineapple, Mango and Oaxacan Chile Sauce (page 34).

1 cup olive oil
1 fresh jalapeño, stemmed
1/3 cup freshly squeezed lemon juice
1 teaspoon salt
1 teaspoon black pepper
8 boneless chicken breasts (skin on)

Add oil, jalapeño, lemon juice, salt and pepper to blender; pulse until mixture is chunky but mixed well.

Pour over chicken breasts and let sit in fridge overnight. I like to use chicken breasts with the skin on.

Grill skin-side down on very hot coals. Cook until skin is crispy. Turn over and cook until done.

Yield: 4–6 servings

Smoked Chicken Enchiladas

Here at Eldorado Grill we smoke our own chickens. It's not necessary to do this, but—man—it sure makes a difference in the flavor.

Filling:
1 pound smoked chicken meat, chopped
1 pound roasted chicken meat, chopped;
*   (meat picked from a whole roasted*
*   chicken is best)*
1 teaspoon garlic, chopped
2 teaspoons fresh ground cumin seed
2 teaspoons salt
1/2 bunch green onions, chopped
1 tablespoon Chipotle Purée (page 28)
3/4 pound Monterey Jack cheese, grated
1/2 pound cream cheese, softened

16 softened corn tortillas (page 14)
Additional Monterey Jack cheese, grated
Sauce or salsa of choice

Preheat oven to 425 degrees.

Gently combine all filling ingredients in a large mixing bowl. Be careful not to break down the meat too much.

Fill softened corn tortillas and roll into enchiladas. Top with Monterey Jack cheese and bake at 425 degrees for 25 minutes. (See rolling and grilling tips on page 14.) I prefer to grill enchiladas, but they can also be baked.

Serve with the sauce or salsa of your choice.

These can be rolled ahead of time and stored in the refrigerator for up to 3 days.

Yield: 12-16 enchiladas

Lemon Jalapeño Chicken Breast
(pictured) with Blackened Tomato Salsa and mashed potatoes

Chicken, Mushroom and Chile Pasilla Stew

These are the most heavenly flavors together. At Eldorado Grill I use free-range chickens. Each is around six pounds. If you can't find free-range chickens in your area, use two commercial chickens or cut this recipe in half.

1 tablespoon vegetable oil
1 5-pound chicken, cut into 10–12 pieces
1 large yellow onion, diced
2 pounds button mushrooms, sliced
1/2 pound portabella mushrooms, sliced
10 cloves garlic
2 tablespoons salt
1 tablespoon black pepper
1 1/2 pounds russet potatoes,
*   peeled and cut into cubes*
2 quarts chicken stock
5 tablespoons chile pasilla flakes
Chopped cilantro
Fresh corn tortillas

Heat oil in a large cast iron skillet, sauté pan or Dutch oven. Cook chicken pieces until very brown. Add onion, mushrooms, garlic, salt and pepper; cook until tender and brown.

Add potatoes, chicken stock and chile pasilla flakes; bring to a boil. Reduce heat and simmer for about 2 1/2 hours.

Serve in bowls with chicken, potatoes and broth. Garnish with fresh cilantro and serve with fresh corn tortillas. Great with a cold, Tecate longneck bottle of beer to wash it all down.

Yield: 1 gallon, about 6 servings

Stuffed Chicken Breast

*Twelve 8-ounce, double-lobed, chicken
breasts with skin on
2–3 ounces Potato and Chorizo Stuffing
per breast (page 46)*

To make a stuffed chicken breast,
place chicken breast, skin side down, on
cutting board covered with a plastic bag.
Pound with a meat mallet until the breast is
about 1/2 inch thick.

Put 2–3 ounces of Potato and
Chorizo Stuffing on chicken breast and fold
in half like a taco. Skewer closed with 8
inch skewers.

Roast in the oven for 35–45 minutes
at 375 degrees, or grill for about 20
minutes, turning often.

*Yield: 10–14 servings. Cut recipe in
half for 4–6 servings*

5 WAYS TO EAT CATFISH

I really like catfish, but for some reason people seem to think it's not a good fish to use for cooking. So, here are a few ways to prepare it that, I think, will change your mind.

Note: Cook your catfish dishes well. It is hard to overcook this fish, and it's better well-done than medium-rare. Medium-rare catfish will turn anybody off, that's for sure!

Blackened Catfish

Lay out the fish fillet and lightly coat with vegetable oil, making sure to coat it completely. Heat your cast iron skillet thoroughly (very hot), then put the fillet in the Blackening Spice Rub (page 45) for only a second. Don't leave it in the spice rub.

Lay fish spice side down in skillet. Don't breathe the smoke. Cook for about 2 minutes; remove and place on sheet pan. Repeat until you have fried all the fillets.

Preheat oven to 450 degrees. Bake fillets for about 15 minutes, until fork tender. At Eldorado Grill we serve Blackened Catfish with Salsa Verde and black beans, Achiote and Chipotle Purées with black-eyed peas and rice.

Chorizo and Yellow Cornmeal Rubbed Catfish (pictured) with Tomatillo Salsa and fresh greens with Lemon-Cumin Vinaigrette

Sundowner Menu

Cocktail—*Tequila Sunset*

•

Starter—*Pico de Gallo with Chips*

•

Entrée—*Four Cheese Chile Relleno
with Shrimp Relish Salad,
Black Beans and Blackened Tomato Salsa*

•

Dessert—*Pepita Pie*

Catfish Mariposa

Lay out the catfish fillets on a lightly oiled sheet pan. Coat with Achiote Purée (page 30), covering completely on top side only. Bake in oven at 450 degrees for about 20–25 minutes or until fork tender.

Place on top of Salsa Verde (page 27) and garnish with Avocado Salad (page 59), Pickled Red Onions (page 43), and Chipotle Purée (page 28), along with fried corn tortillas. Mariposa means *butterfly* in Spanish.

Catfish Mariposa *(pictured)*
Achiote rubbed catfish fillet with fresh avocado, Pickled Red Onions, Black Bean Purée and Chipotle Purée

Blue or Yellow Corn Crusted Catfish

Season 2 cups of cornmeal with salt and pepper to taste. Lightly coat catfish fillet with oil on both sides. Put them in cornmeal mixture and leave them for 5 minutes.

Into a hot skillet, add 2 tablespoons of vegetable oil. Place fillets in pan. (Don't crowd the fish.) Cook on medium heat until fork tender for 5–6 minutes on each side. Place fillets on top of sauce and garnish with salsa or just top with salsa and serve with lemons.

Yield: Covers about 3 pounds of fish fillets or 8–10 6-ounce fillets

Grilled Catfish with Cracked White Pepper

Lay out catfish fillets and lightly coat with vegetable oil. Season with salt and generous amounts of fresh cracked white pepper.

Grill for about 6 minutes on each side. Serve with Lime Cream Sauce (page 35) and Achiote Purée (page 30). Top with Shrimp Relish Salad (page 58), Salsa Verde (page 27) or Ancho Sauce (page 32)— you choose. Always serve with fresh lime wedges.

Blackened Catfish *(pictured)*
with Salsa Verde, Achiote Purée, Black Bean Purée, Avocado Salsa and Pickled Red Onion

Chicken Fried Steak

*1 pound beef tenderloin, cut into
      2-ounce portions*
Salt and pepper
1 cup buttermilk
canola oil
4 cups flour mixture (recipe follows)

Lay out the fillets one at a time and cover with a plastic bag. With a meat mallet, pound them out until they are about 1/4 inch thick.

Lightly salt and pepper them and place in a bowl. Repeat with all fillets. Cover with buttermilk and let them sit in the fridge for at least 30 minutes (overnight is okay, too).

When ready to fry, heat about 1/2 inch of oil in a cast iron skillet to 325 degrees. Press each fillet into the flour mixture and cover completely. Then shake off excess flour and place in oil, 3-4 fillets at a time.

Cook about 3-4 minutes on each side until crispy and golden brown.

Yield: 2–3 servings

Chicken Fried Steak Flour

4 cups flour
1 tablespoon black pepper
1/2 tablespoon cumin
1/2 tablespoon coriander
1/2 tablespoon celery salt
1/2 tablespoon kosher salt
1/2 tablespoon dark chile powder
1 tablespoon cornstarch

Mix all ingredients together in a bowl. Use for chicken fried steak.

Yield: 4 cups

Southwestern Meat Loaf

This meat loaf recipe is traditional, with a Southwestern twist. Like grandma would make, if she lived in Santa Fe.

3 1/2 pounds ground chuck
1 clove garlic, minced
1/4 yellow onion, diced
1/2 tablespoon Dijon mustard
1/2 tablespoon salt
1/2 tablespoon black pepper
1 teaspoon ground cumin
3/4 cup green chiles, diced
1 tablespoon Worcestershire sauce
3 eggs
1/2 cup ketchup
1 cup corn tortillas, cut into
*   1/2 inch squares*

Preheat oven to 400 degrees.

Combine all ingredients in a large mixing bowl. Form into 3/4 pound-loaves and place on a sheet pan. Set aside for about 15 minutes until the loaves come to room temperature.

Bake loaves for 45–55 minutes. Let stand for 10 minutes before slicing and serving.

Yield: Makes 4 loaves

Cochinita Pibil (Achiote Pork Stew)

This dish is a cross between a traditional pork dish from Mexico and good ol' Southern beef stew. The Mexican version is made with banana leaves and no vegetables. It's great for an easy meal and on cold winter nights. You can also make this in a crock-pot. Start it in the morning and it will be ready after work!

5 pounds pork butt, cut into 3-inch cubes
1 cup Achiote Purée (page 30)
1 1/2 pounds russet potatoes, peeled and
*   cut into 2-inch cubes*
2 pounds baby carrots
1 large onion, chopped
1 quart chicken stock
10 cloves garlic
1 tablespoon fresh ground cumin
1 tablespoon black pepper
1 tablespoon salt

Combine all ingredients in a large roasting pan or Dutch oven. Cover and place in 400 degree oven. Bake for 1 3/4 hours.

Uncover and bake for an additional hour or until pork is fork-tender. If using a crock-pot, cook on low for 5–6 hours.

Yield: Serves 10–14 people. Cut recipe in half for 6 people.

Tips on Fish—from the Publisher

Our oceans are in trouble. Ninety percent of the large predator fish—swordfish, marlin, shark, cod, tuna—are gone, fished out. Two-thirds of the 200 or so commercially fished species aren't harvested in a sustainable manner. More fish are caught than can be replaced.

"When I was a chef in Texas, I saw red fish become scarce until it was no longer available. I decided it was up to me to serve fish and seafood in my restaurant that is caught in a way that ensures the population will continue.

I always offer farm-raised catfish to my customers, because it's tasty, fresh and low on the food chain. I don't need swordfish or snapper to make an excellent dish.

I prefer mahi mahi (common dolphin fish), ono (also called wahoo), and U.S.–caught shrimp from the Gulf of Mexico.

—Executive Chef Kevin Tubb

Shrimp farms pollute the coastline and nurseries of wild fish. Foreign-caught shrimp is trawled by ships that kill a lot of by-catch (unwanted species) including sea turtles, marine mammals and sea birds.

As a consumer, you can make a difference. Ask for responsibly caught fish and seafood.

Bad choices include Atlantic cod, Atlantic or farmed salmon, Chilean sea bass, grouper, orange roughy, shark, swordfish and snapper.

Good choices include wild-caught Alaska salmon, Alaska halibut, tilapia, mahi mahi, catfish, oysters, mussels, clams and stone crabs.

Several environmental groups offer tips on seafood that's good for you and good for the ocean. To learn more, see:

www.americanoceans.org
www.blueoceaninstitute.org
www.environmentaldefense.org
www.montereybayaquarium.com
www.oceansalive.org
www.oceanlegacy.org

Tortilla Wrapped Fish with Three Purées

*1 cup canola oil plus 2 tablespoons,
      divided*
8 corn tortillas
*Eight 3-ounce fresh fish fillets (catfish,
      halibut or mahi mahi)*
Salt and pepper to taste

Heat 1 cup of oil in medium-sized skillet over medium heat.

Cook tortillas in oil, one at a time, until soft. Drain on paper towels. Trim each fillet, forming a long triangle. Salt and pepper fillet, place on tortilla, and fold two sides over to form a triangle.

Heat remaining oil over medium-high heat. Place four tortilla triangles, folded side down, in skillet. Cook about 3 minutes on one side, then turn over and cook 2–3 minutes until tortilla is brown and crispy.

Remove from skillet, place in 450 degree oven and bake for about 20 minutes.

To serve, place two tortillas on each plate. Cover tortillas with Lime Cream Sauce (page 35) until they rest in a pool of sauce. Drizzle three purées—Black Bean Purée (page 28), Achiote Purée (page 30), and Chipotle Purée (page 28) over the fillets. Garnish with guacamole.

Yield: 4 servings

Grilled Tortilla Wrapped Fish *(pictured)*
*with Lime Cream Sauce, Achiote, Black Bean
and Chipotle Purées*

Corn Quesadillas

1 pound cooked black beans
2 cups New Mexican green chiles, diced
3/4 pound feta cheese, crumbled
1 pound Monterey Jack cheese, grated
1 teaspoon fresh ground cumin
1/2 teaspoon fresh ground black pepper
1/2 teaspoon salt
1/2 cup corn, fresh grilled and cut off cob
6 tablespoons vegetable oil
24 yellow corn tortillas (see tips on rolling
    and stuffing enchiladas, page 14)
Salt to taste

Combine first 8 ingredients in large mixing bowl.

Soften the corn tortillas (see page 14). Sometimes tortillas are thin. Use 1 thick tortilla and fill with 3–4 tablespoons of mixture. Fold in half. (If the tortillas are thin, I stack 2 tortillas together, then fill and fold.)

Fry with hot oil in skillet until crispy and cheese is melted. Lightly salt.

Yield: 12 quesadillas

Dusty Road Menu

Cocktail—*Ultimate Mezcal Margarita*

•

Starter—*Sopa De Chihuahua*
(the region, not the dog)

•

Entrée—*Grilled Lobster, Shrimp*
and Crab Enchiladas with
Lime Cream Sauce and Chipotle Purée

•

Dessert—*Coconut Ancho Buttermilk Pie*

Pasilla Chicken Enchiladas

1 roasted or boiled chicken, meat picked
from the bone and shredded
1/2 cup pasilla chile flakes
1/2 teaspoon salt
1/2 teaspoon black pepper
1/4 cup white vinegar
8 ounces cream cheese, softened
12–15 corn tortillas

Combine all ingredients except tortilla in a bowl. Roll into enchiladas (see page 14.)

Grill or bake at 425 degrees for 25 minutes.

Yield: 12 to 15 enchiladas

Cheese and Spinach Enchiladas

Vegetarians will clamor for these tasty enchiladas.

1 pound frozen spinach
1/4 pound feta cheese, crumbled
1/2 pound white cheddar cheese, grated
1/2 pound goat cheese, at room temperature
1/4 cup freshly squeezed lime juice
3 green onions, sliced
1 teaspoon fresh marjoram
1/2 teaspoon white pepper
12 corn tortillas

Thaw and drain spinach. Spread spinach on a sheet pan and bake for about 30 minutes so it's really dry. Let cool.

Combine all other ingredients except tortillas in a mixing bowl.

Mix in the spinach. Chill for a couple of hours.

Stuff tortillas and grill or bake at 425 degrees for 25 minutes. (See tips on page 14.)

Yield: 12 enchiladas

DESSERTS

Kevin's Perfect Pie Crust

2 1/2 cups all-purpose flour
1 teaspoon salt
1 teaspoon sugar
2 sticks unsalted butter, chilled and
    cut into pieces
4 tablespoons ice water

Mix flour, salt and sugar in a medium bowl. Using a pastry blender, cut butter into dry mixture. Mixture should resemble corn meal.

Add ice water; work with hands until dough comes together. If dough is still too crumbly, add more ice water, one teaspoon at a time. Do not overwork.

Divide dough in half and flatten into disks. Wrap disks separately in plastic—refrigerate at least one hour.

To form the pie shell, roll the dough on a floured surface into a 14-inch round. Wrap around rolling pin and carefully place over a 9-inch pie pan. Press to fit pan, crimp edges.

To par-bake crust, cut parchment paper and place it to fit over the dough. Fill with a layer of dry beans. (The beans hold the pie crust flat while baking.) Bake at 375 degrees for 10–12 minutes.

Yield: 2 9-inch pie crusts

Chocolate Ancho Pecan Pie

1/4 pound butter
7 eggs
1 cup sugar
1/4 cup Ancho Purée (page 9)
1 tablespoon vanilla extract
1 cup corn syrup
4 cups toasted pecan pieces
1/2 pound semi-sweet chocolate chips
2 par-baked pie shells (page 107)

Preheat oven to 375 degrees.

Melt butter and set aside in mixing bowl.

Combine eggs, sugar, Ancho Purée, vanilla and corn syrup in separate mixing bowl.

Combine butter and egg mixture. Add pecans and chocolate chips. Pour into two 9-inch par-baked pie shells.

Bake for about 50 minutes, until center is just firm and pie is golden brown. Serve at room temperature.

Yield: 2 9-inch pies

Chocolate Ancho Pecan Pie *(pictured)*
with Vanilla Bean Ice Cream and Tequila
Crème Anglaise

Josh's Pecan Pie

This is the best pecan pie I've ever had. (Relatives should disregard that statement.)

4 eggs
1/2 cup light corn syrup
1/4 cup sugar
1/4 cup brown sugar
1/8 cup honey
1/8 cup molasses
1/2 level tablespoon kosher salt
1/2 tablespoon vanilla extract
1/8 pound melted butter
1/4 ounce Kahlua
1/4 ounce bourbon
3 cups toasted pecan halves
1 par-baked pie shell (page 107)

Preheat oven to 375 degrees.

Combine all ingredients in a large mixing bowl. Pour into 9-inch par-baked pie shell.

Bake for about 50 minutes; until center is just firm and pie is golden brown. Serve at room temperature.

Yield: 1 pie

Cinnamon Crème Brulée

1 cup milk
3 cups heavy cream
1/2 teaspoon cinnamon
1 vanilla bean, cut down middle
1 cup sugar
1 cup of egg yolks

You'll need 12-14 three-ounce ramekins (ceramic or Pyrex oven-proof custard dishes) for this recipe.

Preheat oven to 375 degrees.

In large saucepan, scald (boil) milk, cream, cinnamon and vanilla bean.

Beat sugar and egg yolks in small mixing bowl.

Carefully pour egg mixture into saucepan, stirring constantly. As soon as mixture starts to boil, remove from heat and pour through strainer to remove any lumps.

Pour into ramekins and place them in a 2-inch-deep baking pan. Pour warm water around the ramekins about 1/2 way up. Cover pan with foil or lid and bake for 50–60 minutes or until middle is firm. Be careful not to overcook.

Yield: 12 servings

Cinnamon Crème Brulée *(pictured)*

Nanny's Caramel Nut Pie

3 eggs, separated
3 tablespoons flour
1 1/2 cups plus 2 tablespoons sugar,
    divided
1 1/4 cups milk
1 five-ounce can evaporated milk
1 tablespoon plus 1 teaspoon vanilla
    extract, divided
1 cup toasted pecan pieces
1 par-baked pie shell (page 107)

Preheat oven to 325 degrees.

Beat egg yolks in mixing bowl.
Add flour and mix well. Add 1 cup sugar,
milk and evaporated milk. Beat together
and place in double boiler. Heat, stirring
constantly until thickened; should be the
consistency of pudding. Set aside and
keep warm.

Place 1/2 cup sugar in a separate
saucepan over medium heat. Caramelize to
the color of medium to dark brown, being
careful not to burn, and stirring constantly.

Slowly whip the caramelized
sugar into the double boiler mix. Add 1
tablespoon vanilla and pecans; mix well.
Pour into pie shell.

Using a clean, separate mixing
bowl, beat egg whites to soft peaks. Add 2
tablespoons sugar and 1 teaspoon vanilla.
Spread this meringue over pie. Bake pie for
7–10 minutes. Let cool for at least 2 hours.

Yield: 1 pie

Pepita Pie

It's just like a traditional pecan pie, with a south of the border twist.

4 eggs, lightly beaten
1/2 cup light corn syrup
1/4 cup sugar
1/4 cup brown sugar
1/8 cup honey
1/8 cup molasses
1/2 level tablespoon kosher salt
1/2 tablespoon vanilla extract
1/8 pound melted butter
1/4 ounce Kahlua
3 cups pumpkin seeds, toasted, salted and
    finely chopped
1 par-baked pie shell (page 107)

Preheat oven to 375 degrees.

Combine all ingredients in a large mixing bowl. Pour into 9-inch par-baked pie shell.

Bake for about 50 minutes, until center is just firm and pie is golden brown.

Yield: 1 pie

Coconut Cascabel Buttermilk Pie

7 eggs, lightly beaten
3/4 cup sugar
3/4 cup sweet shredded coconut,
    lightly toasted
3/4 cup buttermilk
1/2 teaspoon vanilla
1/4 pound melted butter
2 tablespoons cascabel flakes
1 par-baked pie crust (page 107)

Preheat oven to 350 degrees.

Combine all ingredients in a mixing bowl. Pour into pie shell.

Bake for 45 minutes. Cool, then refrigerate, but let it warm up a bit before serving.

Yield: 1 pie

TEQUILA COCKTAILS

How To's from the Bartender

Eldorado Grill and Tequila Lounge—famous for its tequila cocktails—will set your taste buds to tinglin'. Here are some bartender's tips for the cocktails that follow.

Tip 1. To make *sugar water*, simply combine 1/2 cup sugar with 1/2 cup hot water and chill.

Tip 2. To serve *straight up*, put fresh juices and sugar water in a cocktail shaker. Add all the liquors and about 1 cup of ice and shake vigorously. I repeat, shake vigorously! Pour all ingredients into a martini glass, straining the ice. I don't recommend using a blender.

Tip 3. To serve *on the rocks*, repeat the steps in Tip 2. Instead of straining the ice, just pour all the ingredients into a rocks glass.

Tip 4. To salt your glass rim, run a wedge of lime around the rim of a rocks or martini glass, then press it into a small plate of coarse salt.

Sip and enjoy!

Tito's Typhoon

1 1/2 ounces Tito's Handmade Vodka
(distilled in Austin, Texas)
1 ounce sugar water (page 118)
1 ounce freshly squeezed lime juice
1/2 ounce Pusser's dark rum
1/2 ounce Blue Curacao liqueur

Serve straight up with a twist of lemon.

Eldorado Margarita

1 1/2 ounces 100% agave tequila
3/4 ounce Patron Citronge Premium
*   Triple Sec*
1 1/2 ounces freshly squeezed lime juice
1 ounce sugar water (page 118)

Serve straight up with a lime twist or on the rocks with fresh lime.

Iguana Margarita

1 1/2 ounces Herradura Silver Tequila
3/4 ounce Triple Sec
1/2 ounce Midori Melon liqueur
1 ounce freshly squeezed lime juice
1 ounce sugar water

Serve straight up with a lime twist.

City Slicker

1 1/2 ounces Herradura Silver Tequila
3/4 ounce Chambord liqueur
1 1/2 ounces freshly squeezed lime juice
1 ounce sugar water (page 118)

Serve straight up with a lemon twist.

Shawn's Ultimate Mezcal Margarita

1 ounce Del Maguey Minero Mezcal
1 ounce Grand Marnier
1 1/2 ounces freshly squeezed lime juice
1 ounce sugar water (page 118)

Serve straight up or on the rocks with fresh lime.

Blazing Saddle

1 1/2 ounces chile tequila
3/4 ounce Triple Sec
1 1/2 ounces lime juice, fresh squeezed
1 ounce sugar water

Tip: to make chile tequila, crush some dried chiles into your favorite 100% agave tequila. At Eldorado, we use Oaxacans, cascabels and New Mexican chiles.

Serve straight up or on the rocks with fresh lime.

Shawn's Smoking Gun

2 dashes bitters
1 1/2 ounces chile tequila
1/2 ounce Del Maguey Chichicapa Mezcal
1 1/2 ounces freshly squeezed lime juice
1 ounce sugar water (page 118)

Serve straight up or on the rocks with fresh lime.

Courtin' Cowboy Menu

Cocktail—*City Slicker*

•

Starter—*Tortilla Soup*

•

Entrée—*Catfish Mariposa with Avocado Salad, Pickled Red Onions, Black Bean Purée & Chipotle Purée*

•

Dessert—*Crème Brulée*

Catfish Mariposa *(pictured)*
*with Avocado Salad, Pickled Red Onion,
Black Bean Purée and Chipotle Purée*

Tequila Sunset

1 1/2 ounces Herradura Silver Tequila
3/4 ounce Triple Sec
1/4 ounce Grenadine
2 1/2 ounces orange juice

Serve straight up with a twist of lemon.

From the Author

Born a native Texan, I've always enjoyed the diverse palates of the southwest regions. Here at Eldorado Grill I have been able to mix the flavors I have come to love, using a variety of products from Mexico, New Mexico and Texas. These include annato paste, dried chiles, yellow and blue cornmeals, fresh poblano and serrano peppers, tomatillos, chorizo and more. I have tried to create a food style that complements these flavors in a less traditional form using French techniques in sauce-making, as well as
my own ideas from experiences in the culinary field.

I have been cooking professionally since 1983 and have had the opportunity to work with some of the great chefs from the Southwest who taught me never to compromise on quality, presentation or sanitation. I regularly cooked for Lady Bird Johnson and Governor Ann Richards in Austin, Texas. I relocated to Madison in 1996 and have run Eldorado Grill ever since.

This cookbook is for you. Enjoy it.

—Kevin Tubb, executive chef and proprietor, Eldorado Grill

Index